OVERCOMING YOUR
ANXIETY

FOR PEOPLE ON THE GO

ANDREW CASTRO

Copyright © Andrew Castro 2018

This book is the copyright of Andrew Castro Seishas. No part of this publication may be reproduced, stored in or introduced in a retrieval system without the prior written consent/permission of the copyright owner.

Acknowledgments

First of all, I want to thank you. I want to thank you for having the courage to purchase a book like this and taking a new step in your journey to overcoming your anxiety.

I want to thank my parents. They are always there to support me during my darkest times and my times of joy.

I want to thank Dana for taking time out of her busy life to edit this. I'm sure it wasn't easy.

I want to thank all the authors whose books I have read that inspired me and led me down the path of writing my own book.

And least of all, but I still want to do it, I want to thank myself for having the courage to sit down and pour out my soul on these pages. It was a crazy ride. Don't be afraid to show yourself some love.

Table Of Contents

PART 1 - HOW DID WE GET HERE? 1

    Chapter 1 - My Journey 3

    Chapter 2 - The Snowball, The Wrecking Ball And The Bully Analogies 13

    Chapter 3 - Where Does It Hurt? Symptoms 19

PART 2 - WHERE DO WE GO FROM HERE? 39

    Chapter 4 - Stop Reacting, Start Acting 43

    Chapter 5 - The Mind Makes A Great Slave But A Terrible Master 55

    Chapter 6 - Positivity Vs Productivity 61

    Chapter 7 - Meditation And The Present Moment 65

Some Final Thoughts 75

Afterword 79

Follow Me

Hey you! Yeah, you! So you decided to open up my book. Congratulations on taking this new step on your journey.

Take a second and sign up for my email list here...

www.andrewcastro.net

I will not harass you with daily emails. The emails will come just once a week and here are some of the things you'll get:

New tips and insights on anxiety that aren't in the book

I'll be starting a podcast in October. You will get the episodes the day before they come out.

You'll be notified about public appearances and new products of mine coming out.

Look, you'll be seeing this page in the middle and end of the book so might as well just get it over with

How to use this book

I set out to make this book compact for people on the go. Something that you can throw in your purse or in your backpack or download on your phone, and just go. Go and travel the world or take a road trip with your friends or jump on a cruise ship, you know, all those things you may be putting off because of your anxiety. I mean the book is only like 100 pages. If you can't get through this book maybe reading just isn't your thing.

It's a book written from my own experience and the knowledge I have gained through books, self-reflection and having suffered for many years with anxiety. Though I've conquered so much and made gigantic strides, I'm not totally out of the woods yet which is why I feel I can relate to you right now.

In this book, I will refer to anxiety as a habit quite a bit. Not a habit like biting your nails or clearing your throat, although formed in a similar way, but a psychological habit - a habit of the mind. I have learned that most of my issues with anxiety have come from habits that have formed over many years; most of the time unconsciously. Habits form a lot of what we do and what we avoid. If you're afraid to fly and every time someone invites you on a trip you say no to avoid flying, you're developing a new habit of never getting on a plane. The more something becomes a habit the easier it is to perform whether it is positive or negative. In this book, we will be talking about negative habits that develop and how to consciously change them into more productive habits.

The good news is that habits can be changed or broken. Habits are performed over and over again. They are tended to like a garden and it's up to you which seeds to water and help grow. You might be saying to yourself, "Why would I make scary thoughts or irrational worrying a habit?" Well in a very counter-intuitive way we, I mean for those of us who have anxiety issues, almost enjoy the worrying and negative thinking because they have become our habit. It becomes who we are and we feel there is no other way. It becomes our identity and our safety net. At some point in our lives, we made a choice to think this way and react this way and it became "us."

I'm here to tell you, that as sure as you created these habits you can change them. This book is filled with stories from my life, descriptions of symptoms of anxiety that we all go through and tools and practices that are productive and proactive in creating new and healthier habits. I want to be upfront with you. This is a process that takes time, dedication and courage. It isn't as simple as putting hot sauce on your fingernails to stop biting them. I am going to show you how I was able to see thought patterns and reaction patterns differently and learn how to deal with sensations and irrational thinking. You will learn how to see anxiety as one problem and not 15-20 smaller ones that you are always trying to micromanage. Most of all you will be training and learning to flex the muscle of acceptance.

The word "Overcome" in the title was chosen very carefully. I really dislike it when people use the phrase "Manage your anxiety." In my experience, you can conquer this thing and overcome it. It is true that some sensations and thoughts may pop up from time to time but if you don't pay them any attention or give them fuel anymore then they don't hold anything on you. If something loses its grip on you then you're not managing it anymore. You have become the master of it.

If I had a choice in how you read this book I would say read it all the way through once. Take it in as a whole. Let it sink in for a couple days and then go back to it as needed. Like I said in the beginning, take it with you in your purse or briefcase or jacket pocket. I want it to be your anxiety guide, like people who take those Rick Steves travel books everywhere. Let this be your companion.

I hope I accomplished what I set out to do and I hope my story can help even just one person. Although selling like 10,000 of these would really help my financial situation.

.

PART 1

HOW DID WE GET HERE?

CHAPTER 1

My Journey

I want to start this book by telling you my story. This is important because, as you'll see, aside from the specific situations I found myself in, my reaction and patterns to my thoughts and sensations are going to look very similar to yours. If there was one thing that ignited my dedication to overcome my anxiety it was realizing that I wasn't unique or special, that I wasn't alone in this... you are not alone in this.

I am a pretty normal guy. I am not a doctor, psychologist or psychiatrist and I am certainly no grammar expert or celebrated writer. I was a film major at a state university. I'm a little over five feet ten inches tall and one hundred and fifty pounds. Nothing special. I'm intelligent....sometimes. I can hold my own in debates on a few different topics. My favorite sport is basketball. I love reading like I'm kind of obsessed with it. Oh yeah, and I am a touring singer-songwriter for a living. So I'm also kind of broke most of the time. So you see I'm pretty normal or whatever you want to call it. Now that we have all that out of the way...I've also suffered from that which shall not be named ...haha just kidding (I also love the Harry Potter Books).

I've suffered from ANXIETY!

Actually, it should be suffering from because I'm not quite out of the woods. But I know I have come very far and it no longer holds the power it once had over me.

Ok, let's backtrack. Here is how it started for me.

When I was about four or five years old, I was at the drive-in movies with my parents. I remember sitting in the middle and at some point during the movie, I became very overwhelmed with fear. Being just a child the sensation was quite strong. What caused this you may be wondering? Worried thoughts are what caused this. It was my first experience that I can remember with racing uncontrollable thoughts. These thoughts crept into my head that someday my parents were going to die (That's right I was super existential and edgy at four years old). At the time I was too young to understand that those thoughts would start snowballing. I couldn't understand that what worried me wasn't that my parents or loved ones would pass away at some point. It was that I had no control over the situation, the when and how of it. I didn't like that. Not…one…bit.

At four years old I just cried and told my parents why I was crying. They comforted me best they could and I eventually settled down and my four-year-old brain wandered on to something else. But things were certainly building and already, at just four-years old, a new cycle of thoughts and thinking had started.

There were times after that drive-in movie moment up to my eighth-grade year when worried thoughts would pop into my head. I had times where I really suffered from not being able to control the things around me. This ranged from what other people were thinking of me to how I looked, comparing myself to others. These patterns built for many years. Eventually, my anxiety manifested itself in the form of obsessive, ritualistic tasks, or OCD. Here are some of the interesting things I used to do:

Brush my teeth a certain way. I had to get the toothpaste on perfectly. I had to rinse the bristles a certain way. I had to get the water right down the center of the brush. I'm getting frustrated thinking about it.

I had to check to make sure every door was locked. Numerous times. Many times I'd go back to bed and my mind would start racing asking questions like "Did you check that door properly?" "Was it actually locked or are you remembering incorrectly?" My mind was up to its dirty tricks.

I'd check all the blinds on my windows to make sure they were shut properly. By properly I mean I had to turn the little stick until it clicked five times. I did this so much I broke numerous sets of blinds. My parents didn't like that.

I would have to say a certain prayer every night the exact same way without messing up or I'd have to start over and I wasn't even very religious. So the prayer was just to ease my mind. It had no true meaning behind it. It just made me feel irrationally safe.

That list can go on and on. These were highly frustrating and exhausting tasks. But to me, at the time, they were worth the frustration, or so I thought. It would sometimes take me about 30 to 45 minutes from the time I decided to go to sleep to when I actually went to sleep because of these irrational and meaningless activities. But at the time these things were my safety net. In my head, if I performed these tasks perfectly then everything and everyone would be safe. It felt real and I was afraid to take a stand against it. I was afraid because if I took a stand and something bad happened it would be my fault because I didn't do some strange irrational ritual. It was my way of attempting to control the outcome of events. My anxiety needed a release somehow and these obsessive tasks were it.

Let me be clear on this. I can tell you now that nothing I did from the list above had any bearing whatsoever on my safety or those around me. It just created really poor habits that would continue to snowball in me. I was basically lying to myself about why I was doing these things. I justified the actions in my head to allow myself to keep doing it.

When I look back now, with a lot more clarity, the rationale behind everything is something I chuckle at. Not that I chuckle at it because I think I was foolish or weak, but because I have grown so much from that time. A lot of anxiety stems from a lack of being able to control the outside world. This can manifest itself in strange ways; crazy thoughts, irrational tasks, avoidance behavior. Anxiety plants its seed and we begin to water it.

Let's jump just a little ahead in that eighth-grade year to April 20th, 1999, the day of the infamous Columbine shooting. It rocked the entire nation and my tiny little world. The days that followed the shooting my anxious, worrying mind became fixated on it. I started seeing myself as the shooters. Violent scary thoughts just invaded my mind. And let me be clear about one thing I'm totally the nicest person ever. I was very confused. I had no real desire whatsoever to hurt anyone. Yet here were these horrible and intrusive thoughts bombarding my angst-filled 13-year-old mind. They would pop up and I would react. Then when they were gone all I could think about was how terrified I was that they would come back. I was afraid of a feeling. That type of fear sort of puts you in limbo, disconnected from the present, past and future because you're afraid to feel anything. My fear of not having control of things started to turn into a lot of "what if" thoughts. What if I became the shooter? What if I actually am crazy? I let my anxiety spawn OCD behavior and now what if thoughts were my favorite thing to focus on.

After hiding these thoughts for a couple of weeks I decided I needed to do something. I told my parents I wanted to go to therapy. This, I have to admit, is a little out of the ordinary for a thirteen-year-old. But I was really shaken and I knew my mom saw a therapist so I thought it can't be that bad.

My mom's therapist was a woman, who I will refer to as Ellen and her husband, who I will call James, had a practice in my town. We set up an appointment for me to see James. I got lucky on my first try. He was great. I told him all about what I was feeling and seeing in my head. I told him all about my OCD and those "what if" thoughts.

I then remember a very simple lesson he told me about his struggle with a certain fear. James was terrified of dark places. He was afraid of being able to see around him. He had this fear even in his own house. This was amazing to me because here is a guy who is helping other people with their fears and problems and he has his own. It makes you realize that everyone and I mean everyone has their issues. You don't need to feel so isolated or alone. Anyway,

I digress. So, he was tired of being afraid of the dark. So one day he just grabbed a chair plopped it in the middle of a room, turned the lights off, and sat there for almost an hour. When he felt the fear creep up, as he was sure it would, he pretty much said: "Fuck you, do your worst!" (This is literally what he said to me) He invited this fear, he welcomed it and did it with a big F-bomb which always helps. He refused to let it control him. He took that stand that I was so afraid to take. I remember him telling me that after a while the fear just turned to boredom and he got up and left.

I left that session confident. I knew what I had to do. Although a light went on in my head after that session it would take a long time to implement that in my everyday life. Understanding something intellectually is one thing. Living that and turning it into wisdom is something that takes time, discipline and courage.

So...on to more of my problems!

I went to college and drank a lot. I went on road trips with my friends, drank a lot. After college, I started to write my own songs to cope with a breakup. But all of this was surface stuff. The real carnage was underneath. I felt like I put just enough work into therapy to function and have fun but never really looked at the problem facing me. I was just putting a bandage on a gunshot wound. I was a functional person with anxiety. Well, everything would come to a head when I turned twenty-five and I would remain in a deep battle for well over a year.

I had these mini anxiety attacks while visiting my friend in New York. The drinking and lack of sleep probably didn't help. But I knew something was wrong. It's literally as simple as one thing led to another and the shit hit the fan. It didn't take long for these little attacks to become an ordeal. Every little task became a little more challenging because I had these overwhelming sensations and terrifying thoughts about them. My world flipped upside down. I didn't want to go out, go on road trips, or do anything that involved any sort of activity at all. My focus was 100% on these powerful sensations that just felt like an electric current through my body. Why they were there? I went to the doctor and he threw a couple Xanax at me to take as needed for general anxiety. It helped at times but I didn't want to become this pill. I didn't want to have a crutch the rest of my life. I knew there had to be another way. Medicine has its place for sure. It just wasn't for me. I was searching endlessly on blogs for answers. I'd type in every symptom and read what people did for that specific thing. This was now my world. How do I solve this problem? I was convinced I was losing it, going nuts. My family would just have to come to visit me in the mental ward.

I stumbled upon this one blog that mentioned a book called *At Last a Life* by Paul David. I didn't know if a book could help me but I bought it. From the first page of this book, I was hooked. It spoke to me. It was one epiphany after another. The symptoms were familiar, the pounding adrenaline was common, the racing thoughts didn't mean I was going crazy. It gave me the acronym FEAR, Face

Everything And Recover. This is what my therapist was saying all along from that lesson about sitting in the dark. It's not that I wasn't facing these things, it was that I was so used to my style of living my habits. I didn't truly understand what I was doing to myself or what I actually needed to face. I quit drinking and told myself I'm going to try and go out and do everything I used to do. Alcohol just exacerbated the problems. I did it and it worked. However, I only did it until I started feeling good again on the surface. I did it until I could start partying and drinking with my friends again. I did not stick to it, but went right back into worrying constantly about things that were out of my control. I would snap at the most insignificant things. I hadn't stopped the snowball I merely slowed it down and it was now starting to pick up even more speed.

Time passed, and after a more than one-year battle with anxiety attacks, generalized anxiety, racing thoughts and depression, I went out with my friends. We were out until 4am drinking. I got in bed at 5am and shot awake at 7am. I saw stars, my heart was racing, adrenaline was surging (Are you feeling a little anxiety just reading this?). I called my parents, I called my girlfriend, I knew this feeling and what it caused me in the past. I was terrified. That terror ignited the old fear of having those overwhelming sensations and scary thoughts. Just the fear that it was coming back was enough to ignite the cycle once again.

That next day was the Super Bowl. I had friends over and I was in no condition to be hospitable. I sat there watching the game just screaming on the inside. That night set off a chain of events that unraveled me again. This time new symptoms popped up like depression and insomnia. These almost caused me not to go to Europe with my family. The fear of the fear was back. Every moment I was walking on glass. When I was relaxed, which was rare, I was searching for the anxiety, anticipating it, knowing it was lying in wait. I had scary thoughts of hurting people I loved, scary thoughts of hurting myself. I never acted on these thoughts but they felt so real, like I was one step away from losing my life. I knew I wasn't this person, I just knew it. But it had a hold of me. The drinking and late nights were just things that intensified everything, they weren't the true problem. I was neglecting myself. By that I mean literally not taking care of my mental and physical faculties. There was no change in my behavioral patterns. There was no change in the habits I had created. If I worked myself into an anxiety attack then that's just what I did without any self-reflection as to why I was doing it. I ignored it because I either thought that's just the way I am or I was too afraid to face it.

Now, this next thing will sound strange to hear but this is truly where I am. Turns out that night before the Super Bowl was one of the great nights of my life. It led me to write this book. It led me to find meditation and self-improvement. It taught me how to be a better person and truly change my behavioral patterns. Most of all it showed me the way of helping others who suffer from the same thing.

Anxiety is a habit, yes a habit, a behavioral cycle that that has trapped you. From here on out, I want you to know that we are going to be dealing with anxiety; not something a doctor can x-ray or take a blood test to figure out. Maybe your anxiety is caused by something a medical doctor can diagnose. If it is that is great because you can take steps to treat it. But then we aren't talking about the same thing. Everything you're feeling is caused by anxiety and that anxiety is caused by fear and that fear is caused by behavioral patterns and habitual tendencies that you thought were just the way you are. But it can be another way. I'll try and show you.

CHAPTER 2

The Snowball, The Wrecking Ball And The Bully Analogies

So now that you know a little about me and my struggles, let's figure out how I got myself into this horrible mess. I am going to apply three simple analogies. The first is a very cliché expression known as the Snowball Effect. I want to use this because it's familiar and visually very helpful.

It comes from the act of taking a small snowball and rolling it down a hill of. As the snowball rolls and picks up momentum, it collects more and more snow, making it grow in size, and increase in intensity and speed. Presumably, at the bottom of the hill, it will crash and explode into a shower of icy particles. Sounds scary, but then again sometimes we have to hit that bottom and crash to begin to rebuild.

Ok so we have that down and I've scared you. Now let's apply.

Most of us start with no snowball or at least it's a very small snowball. There are studies that show genetics can play a part in giving us a predisposition to harboring anxious feelings and thoughts. This is not a death sentence; I wouldn't have written this book if it were. (I won't be going into genetics because that's a whole other book for a much more intelligent person to write.) I am here to speak from my experience dealing with anxiety that is self-inflicted.

So, we are all pretty much born with no snowball. When that little tiny, seemingly insignificant snowball first develops, as it did for me when I was a four-year old at the drive-in movie with my parents, it's either too small to care about or you are too young to understand what is happening. As I got older, worried thoughts would manifest themselves as compulsions, which would create a false safety net. By this point, I had already unknowingly given the snowball a slight nudge to get it rolling down the hill. As the snowball starts rolling, it's basically on autopilot.

I was so caught up in my problems, chronic worrying, racing thoughts, overwhelming sensations of dread, that I really didn't notice the giant snowball picking up speed. You may think, at the time, that you are doing the right thing by trying to solve what you see as a problem. In reality you're ignoring the serious issues that are staring you right in the face: overthinking, compulsion, self-diagnosis and avoidance. WELCOME TO THE SNOWBALL!

You're feeding off that snowball. Or maybe to put it better you're feeding that snowball. Your anxiety isn't something that has always been there. It's not a static thing, you pulled a little from the habit of worrying, a little from irrational safety nets, a little from needing control. You get the picture. All these ingredients become too much for your mind and body to take and then the stress just builds and explodes.

What your mind and body need is to heal. The only way to heal is to get the hell out of the way and allow them to heal. Trust me, I know this sounds so counterintuitive, which is what makes it so difficult. We see a threat and we fight. In the case of anxiety, when you feel it, be aware of it, recognize it, say hello to it and welcome it to the party. Just allow it to be there (we will learn how to do this later). The fighting is the same thing you've been doing for years and it just makes the snowball bigger and bigger and harder and harder to stop. All these different symptoms are just screaming at you and you can't see or think clearly. So here comes my second totally amazing analogy:

The Anxiety Wrecking Ball:

I tried to think of a more pleasant sounding analogy but I couldn't so just deal with it.

The Anxiety Wrecking Ball is a way to look at all your symptoms with more clarity. You with anxiety, then all of the sudden, you have all these crazy symptoms like headaches that you think are tumors, pains in your stomach that you think are cancerous, depression and exhaustion and a myriad more. So just like me, I'm sure you start trying to tackle all of these problems individually, instead of saying it's anxiety. You list your problems, individually, when you tell someone how you're feeling. Here is where the anxiety wrecking ball comes into play.

Close your eyes for a moment, but wait until after you read this paragraph or that wouldn't make much sense. Imagine a giant wrecking ball and the words ANXIETY written on it. Picture a big tall concrete building. Now imagine that wrecking ball swinging right into the building creating a giant crack. It swings again and creating another crack causing new structural problems each time it hits. It just keeps swinging and swinging causing new and different.

You see, there are multiple problems with the building but they are all caused by the same thing. If you keep trying to patch up every little new problem in the building without dealing with the actual cause of the cracks you'll never heal because the wrecking ball will just keep swinging. If you can deal with the wrecking ball and get it to stop then eventually no new problems will be created. It is much easier to fix those cracks if your wrecking ball isn't slamming against the building.

It's a crude analogy, but it gets the point across. Stop dealing with all these symptoms individually and realize the issue is anxiety.

By using the wrecking ball analogy and condensing your problems to one thing you've applied an awareness to your situation that will, in turn, begin to slow down that snowball. For me, this was a huge weight lifted off my shoulders. I realized that my myriad of problems were stemming from one thing. By cutting away all that extra baggage, my focus sharpened and I could apply new productive habits to just one problem instead of ten or twenty individual ones and do it with more clarity.

The last analogy I'll use is short and to the point.

The Bully:

I used to look at my anxiety as a big bully. Of course, we all know what keeps the bully going, right? Your reaction. Bullies love to poke and prod and instigate and cause chaos. The more you give them to feed off of the better. Have you ever seen those movies where one day a kid stands up to the bully because they've had enough? Be that kid. You'll notice that the more you face the bully and don't react to their shenanigans, the more they fade away and lose their power over you. Whenever that bully would creep up on me I'd just invite it in. Let it put on its bully shoes and start stomping away. I'd stick my chin out and just entice that bully to take a swing at me. I would even talk to the bully and say things like, "Come on in, my house is your house" or "Do what you have to do. I'm going to continue reading my book, so have fun" or even "Come on in man let's hang out. The door is open anytime 24/7."

A huge moment for me was when all my friends were going on a trip to Chicago. When I got the invite I was scared to say yes, initially, because of how I felt. I took a breath and just said, "I don't care what you do to me, I'm going on this trip and you can come along or not. I'm going". I stood my ground, went on the trip, felt shitty and had a great time. It sounds weird and scary. Yes the sensations were awful, but the bully eventually ran out of steam. The bully just gets bored and walked away. That same bully may return with a vengeance but now you're not afraid to stand up to it and that's a start. You've now flexed a little baby acceptance muscle (but no one is impressed with that). We want that bulging bicep acceptance muscle.

You only have so much adrenaline in your body at any given moment and by allowing that adrenaline to burn out you've released some of that anxiety. More importantly, you've gained a little ounce of a very powerful thing...confidence.

Confidence turns into belief and faith in yourself and what you have accomplished. I'm a sports fan so I use the analogy when a team wins its first championship (like my beloved Golden State Warriors in 2015) they learned how to win. So next time they are in that situation they know what needs to be done. It is the same with applying these analogies. You'll gain a confidence and belief over time the more you do it. Even if it means that you have to fail a lot to get it right.

There's nothing anxiety hates more than awareness and acceptance. Taking action is anxiety's worst enemy.

CHAPTER 3

Where Does It Hurt? Symptoms

There are two events in my life where I realized that understanding my symptoms could be the most important step toward igniting my recovery and implementing new and productive habits into my life.

The first moment occurred a few years back. I was struggling with every symptom you could think of with my anxiety. I would go on long walks by myself and just cry because I felt I had just become a different person and lost my old self forever. I really didn't want to be here because it was all just too much. My only relief from these symptoms was going to sleep.

In the fog of panic and desperation, I stumbled upon a blog. Can't remember the name of that blog but I remember that someone wrote about a book called *At Last a Life* by Paul David (I mentioned this book earlier so you should probably go out and get it as well). Then I saw in the comments on the book that people were raving about it. I bought the book right there on the spot and it arrived a few days later. Early on in the book the author listed about 15 symptoms of anxiety and I could literally put a checkmark after each one. I was now fully engaged in the pages (Interestingly enough the more I was engaged in reading the book I didn't even notice my anxiety. We seem to not remember those points in our life even though that proves how much focusing on anxiety keeps you from enjoying the life you're living). The parts that hit home the most were the stories from other people who were experiencing the exact same things as me. I'm talking down to the minutest details. We weren't in the exact same situations, but the feelings and emotions were identical. It was like a light switch went on. I wasn't alone. I wasn't going crazy. This was all caused by behaviors, habits, and adrenaline. Knowing that you're not alone is such a weight off your shoulders. Some 40 million people in the United States alone suffer from some form of an anxiety disorder. Your anxiety is not unique.

The other situation came just a few months before writing this book. As I mentioned, I am a touring singer-songwriter. I was on tour in Hawaii and I got a call from a close friend early in the morning. I knew he had been struggling with anxiety again so I answered and we talked for about an hour. I just listened and gave input where I felt I needed to. I was currently still dealing with my own anxiety issues but was definitely making progress.

As he listed everything that was going on in his life it started to feel like I was listening to myself talk about my own anxiety. He described: irrational thoughts, hurting people he loved, racing thoughts, feeling detached, fighting it all and wanting it to go away! I stopped and just told him it was amazing how much alike people are. We are made of the same stuff. Everything he said I have felt personally. I told him I know many others who describe the exact same things. Again, we are not alone.

We tend to think we are so different, that our problems are completely our own. We internalize everything and spend so much time in our own minds that we forget there are other people with the same or worse problems. We tend to isolate ourselves and develop a little self-pity that helps us justify how we feel. As harsh as this sounds...you are not special. Your anxiety is not special, your sensations are not special, they're just not, no matter what your mother tells you. Self-pity doesn't help anyone, especially you. It drags you down and keeps you down. We gather sympathy from people around us and want them to actually affirm our thoughts of being lost and hopeless. Now my friend wasn't looking for pity at all, he was looking to learn. I told him that the fact that we are having this conversation and I can personally, through lived experience, understand what he is talking about, shows that these symptoms might be more common than he initially thought. He just wanted them to go away and it's just not that simple. I told him they can go away through hard work and dedication. But more importantly, they can be transformed. So again, you are not alone in the way you feel and that is a fact.

So, as I list these symptoms I want you to try and look at each one differently. Try not to think that you have it worse or that there is no way out. Listing these symptoms is just a way to show you that you are not alone. I have suffered from everything you suffer from. I am giving you proof that these symptoms aren't unique. Take a breath and let's explore these crazy little symptoms.

Hopefully, after this chapter, you'll feel a little more confident in taking your first steps towards becoming the new and improved you. I'm going to start and end with the two most common symptoms that I dealt with and it seems to be the same for others as well.

Depersonalization/Derealization:

This is a big one and it's probably the hardest to identify because who the hell has actually ever heard of depersonalization. But it is real and isn't all that pleasant. Depersonalization is the feeling of detachment. It's a dreamlike feeling that causes you to disengage from your surroundings. At times you'll feel almost separate from your body. This happened to me a lot towards the end of the day because my mind was just exhausted from running in circles all day. That creates that detached feeling. Personally, I would get a sort of foggy haze to my vision and feel a bit disoriented. Confusion can set in and you feel like you aren't in control of yourself. It's almost like you're watching some weird movie of your life that you would give two thumbs way down. These feelings can make you feel very anxious because it's terrifying to not feel like you are not actually a part of your body and mind. If you let it run wild it can cause a full-blown panic attack. This is a tough symptom especially when it happens in social settings because you feel very helpless. It's an out of body experience, except not the cool kind all those people talk about who go to Burning Man.

What you have to realize here and now is that this is a product of your anxiety. It's a product of your snowball speeding down the hill and manifesting itself through these sensations. When depersonalization happens, identify it, know what it actually is now because I have told you and you can even look it up on the internet. Once our brain understands something a little better it takes the fear of the unknown out.

Know that it passes if you give it space to pass. By identifying it you are taking away a lot of the power it had as an unknown symptom. But you must allow it to run its course because fighting will make it stronger. Don't be afraid of it because it can't hurt you if YOU don't let it. Dive right into it and learn to accept it as your current reality for now. There's no way to ignore it. Besides, ignoring it is almost the same as fighting it. But remember, there is a fine line between ignoring something and accepting it. Ignoring it is just pretending not to notice it in hopes that it will go away. Accepting it is truly being aware of your current state and eventually becoming ok with it.

Exhaustion:

I thought I must have some sort of infection or virus because I was always so tired. Nope! Not the case (although it doesn't hurt to go to the doctor to check in on this). Once you get negative results, you should know this, too, is all because of that jackass, anxiety. You see you're exhausted all the time because you're going twelve rounds a day with anxiety. You're fighting it every moment. Do you think your brain doesn't get tired like any other muscle? Excessive overthinking and worrying cause your exhaustion. You have fixated your focus so hard on your anxiety that you're running on empty all day every day. Your brain needs a rest. It needs to refuel. Try to engage in activities that peak your interest. Try exercise and meditation. Take your focus off yourself and your issues. Give your brain some space to rest. Practicing acceptance is vital as well. If you truly accept something then you're ok with it. If you're ok with it then you're not fighting it.

Headaches:

This symptom can go hand in hand with exhaustion. I thought numerous times I had some sort of incurable brain tumor. When you have anxiety you forget how common headaches are. Well, they are even more common when you're fighting your own thoughts all the time and trying to change everything to your liking. Sometimes you're just going to think crazy weird thoughts. The brain is a data collector and it has little bias on what it collects. It's really just up to you where you are putting your energy and attention.

So sometimes weird shit gets in there. Again your brain needs a little R & R. You need to allow things to pass and stop fixating and engage in more productive activities. If I am making it sound simple that's because it is simple to do these things. The hard part is making them habitual. The hard part is having dedication and perseverance. Every once in a while just take a breath and relax into that headache.

This is Me Forever:

This is one of those thoughts that can really scare you. You feel trapped and almost claustrophobic in your own body. This specific thought symptom can cause a lot of anxiety because it gives that real sense of hopelessness. You want so badly to be the person you were before the anxiety, that you make yourself worse. You're trying to force it away. That is the same as fighting it. It took years for you to get yourself in this mess and it will take time to get out of it (not necessarily years though). I always applied the logic that if I was one way before the anxiety then I can be that way again or perhaps a new and better me. I also looked at moments where I did feel good, which were few and far between, but those moments showed me that anxiety isn't a linear static thing. It fluctuates, and those little bursts of light taught me to be patient and know that if I allow these feelings to pass then the next time they come they will hold less and less power over me because I've been through it. This is not you forever. Try saying that instead. You can't ignore these symptoms because they are real. But you certainly can choose to not give them your full attention.

Everything has its opposite. If your heart is broken from a relationship, well it means it was loved. If someone passes and you're sad, it means you loved them. If you're feeling negative and depressed then you must've known what it was like to not feel that way or how could you decipher the difference between the two.

"What if" Thoughts:

As I mentioned earlier in the book this was a tough one for me because I wanted to have control of things. Basically a "what if" thought is asking the question to yourself "What if this or that happens?" and you can't do anything about it. I have an easy fix for you...

Just wait and see *IF* it happens in the first place and deal with it accordingly and that is all.

Thoughts that you're going crazy:

Been here, had these too. This one really hit me hard because again you feel like you're losing touch with reality and the person you used to be. You start thinking, you're going to have to go live in a mental institute and live in a little white room. Or you need some emergency trip to the ER. It gets even worse when you are out of town or staying in an unfamiliar place. "Do they have an ER out here?" "Are we even near civilization?" "What if I need help and no one can get to me?".

What is actually happening is you are projecting what you think going crazy is and making it seem real. You're worrying so much about going crazy that you're making yourself believe you are. Look back and read that sentence again. You're not going crazy believe me. What you have is adrenaline pumping everywhere because you're always on edge. That adrenaline then feeds into your thoughts, which in turn produce racing scary thoughts like "I'm going crazy". If you really look deep at the thought, you are actually more scared of just the thought of going crazy. I don't think I ever truly believed I was going crazy. I just didn't like the thought of going crazy.

It was a matter of facing these thoughts and recognizing what they are and then not dwelling but engaging in the present moment as best I can. I also really stopped sometimes and looked at who I truly was underneath all the debris of anxiety. I saw a kind person, a genuine person, a loving person, maybe a little lost but truly I saw a good decent person. Remind yourself of who you really are sometimes and allow those scary thoughts to just burn out even if you burst into tears because of it. I remember crying when I truly saw myself underneath. I truly saw a strong, kind person who wouldn't hurt anyone. It's ok to cry, especially at something beautiful like that.

Sleep Trouble:

This symptom can really rock you at your core. Sleep is so important for mental health. For years anxiety never affected my sleep patterns. I remember I was in New York playing some shows and I was staying at my friend's apartment in Manhattan. This was right in the middle of one of my bouts with anxiety. One night it just kind of came out of nowhere. I just couldn't go to sleep. It felt like there was an electrical current just running through my body for a very long time. I finally did go to sleep around 4 or 5 am and had to wake up early the next day to catch my flight home. I was so exhausted and just wanted to get the hell out of New York and back home. Well, as we know exhaustion is also an agitator of anxiety. When I got to my seat on the plane I could feel sensations building. And then there it was, a full-blown anxiety attack. I wanted to get off the plane and just run. I didn't know what to do. I felt trapped. I just thought to myself that this will pass. And of course, it did because adrenaline always burns out. The strange part about the whole attack is that right after it settled, I just felt a strong feeling of bliss. On the other side of this fear lies peace and relaxation. We just have to see through that invisible wall of fear. However, when I got home, I had another sleepless night and then another. This went on for a couple months and it was brutal.

This was a clear result of buying into my thoughts. This was a little sleep snowball that was now forming. One night made me fear it would happen again the next night and the next. I was now just setting myself up for failure. I was sabotaging my present moment (I'll speak on this later). Your body wants to fall asleep. It is made to fall asleep. It is part of our programming. So we are basically just telling ourselves we can't fall asleep because we have anxiety.

When we start to make sleeping a thought process we will never get good sleep because that is not what sleep is. If your mind wants to race at night just let it. The more you get frustrated and buy into what your mind is spewing out the more that sleep snowball will build.

I would get so frustrated and just get up and start cursing because I was so angry at myself, at the world, at these sensations. This only exacerbated the problem. My girlfriend at the time had some sleep trouble as well and would just say, "Why are you getting so frustrated? If you can't sleep just get up or read a book and stop forcing and fighting it. Just accept you are this person right now" She was spot on. Now when I have trouble sleeping, as we all do, even people who aren't big anxiety sufferers, I just think ok I can't sleep right now so let's read a book. After a few moments, my mind will drift back into sleep mode and I will fall asleep much easier than if I used my old methods of getting pissed and frustrated. Remember we have to trust our bodies and minds sometimes to do what they are made for.

Trouble Breathing:

Not sure how many people suffer from this one but I did so I figure someone else has as well.

This symptom was just kind of annoying. I would always think "Oh am I breathing right? Is this good? Am I getting full breaths?" Again this was just me over thinking and getting in my own way. Breathing is just like sleep. Your body will do this for you if you just allow it. Sometimes we need to take bigger breaths to relax or after climbing a staircase, but most of the time breathing should be left to its own devices. It was just another trick played on me by my thoughts. I knew this because I might go two or three hours without even noticing my breath and then as soon as I put some attention on it for some strange reason it was all I thought about. I began to see that trick clearly. So when my mind tried to tell me something was wrong with my breathing I would say "Well what about all that time before this thought where I didn't even think about it? What about then?" The mind is a crazy magician. You just have to see through its trickery. When you were born did you have trouble breathing? The answer is no because you weren't thinking about it. You're just getting in your own way. Science and personal experience can both guarantee that your lungs will take in oxygen and release carbon dioxide for you. Don't fall for the tricks.

Feeling anxious and nervous for absolutely no reason:

Sometimes I'd just be sitting there and I would just have a burning sensation all over. Adrenaline would just be pumping. I would squirm and fight and just want to be out of the situation. But I did that for years and years and it just made things worse. Nothing seemed to get better. This can be extremely uncomfortable. Once the adrenaline starts pumping the fear sets in or the other way around it doesn't matter. The adrenaline feeds into your thoughts, your thoughts scare you and in turn feed right back into the adrenaline. This is exhausting and draining. As well it should be. What else do you think is supposed to happen when you're fighting something all day every day? Fighting is exhausting, letting go is a relief. Here is an example analogy from my life:

When I sit down to write a song I put a lot of focus into it. But when I sit down for an hour or two and I'm still on the same song, I know there's a problem. The lyrics aren't coming out, the melody is all over the place. My brain starts to hurt. I get very frustrated and worst of all, with all the focus I am putting into it, the song is going nowhere. It's actually only causing problems. I have learned now that I need to just get up and walk away from the song. I recognize the issue and take a step back to see that all this fighting and forcing my energy into the situation is making things worse. During that time that I just let go of the song for a bit, I gain so much clarity. The weight of that song is immediately taken off my shoulders when I stop fighting it. And you know what? During my little refreshing break seems to be the time when the melody and lyrics come to me. Sometimes focus, even on good positive things, can drain you. So imagine how bad you'll feel when you're focused on negative unproductive things.

Scary Violent Thoughts:

These type of thoughts scared me the most and came out of nowhere. Scary violent thoughts, especially when you're not a violent person, can be very disturbing. The strange thing is that the violent thoughts would almost always be about people I loved like parents, girlfriend, friends, myself. I had a real problem being around knives. Every time I was in sight of a knife with someone I loved near me, I got some crazy thought of hurting them. This terrified me. I thought I was turning into a psychopath. It wasn't just knives though. When I got close to edges I was afraid I'd jump. When people I knew were close to edges I was afraid I'd push them. These were all very disturbing. It's no coincidence that the feelings and sensations that come with fear cause violent and terrifying thoughts.

A few things really opened my eyes. One was knowledge. I began to read other people's stories and they had the same exact problems. My friend that I mentioned before, told me about his thoughts of hurting people he loved. This showed me that I wasn't losing it. There is clearly a common theme going on here. Another thing that helped me was actually opening up to the people I was having the thoughts about. I told my parents and my girlfriend. They didn't look at me like I was crazy. In fact, my girlfriend told me "Well that's ok. I want to let you know that I feel completely safe around you." I just started crying when she said that (Ok, I cried a lot during this process- I get it) Hearing the perspective of someone I respect and love say that after what I just told her was very moving. Your family is there to support you. And if they aren't or you feel you have no support then this book is here, I am here, there are groups out there made up of people that are feeling the same as you. You are never alone.

The last thing that helped me was that these thoughts were mainly happening around people I love. There must be something to this. I analyzed this and did little tests like trying to think the same thoughts about some random person walking down the street. You know what happened? Not that much, It didn't feel quite the same. I reflected on this. I began to understand that my anxiety was feeding off my deepest fears. You see anxiety feeds off your stress and your negativity and your fears and whatever you feed it. What could give you or me more fear and stress than having thoughts of hurting the people we hold closest to us? I began to see anxiety's dirty little tricks. It made me a little angry because it made me second-guess the type of person I truly was. So a big fuck you to anxiety for that one.

So when these thoughts arose in my head I would invite them and say "Do your worst my friend but I know I would never, ever do those things". In reality, the strong violent thoughts I was having, were really a form of love for those people. That sounds very strange to hear but it's true. You love these people so much that the most terrifying thing you can think of would be to hurt one of them. These thoughts are false. They are waves of adrenaline mutating into thoughts that are feeding off deep dark fears of becoming something or someone you are not. You know you are not this person. So go ahead and show those thoughts that they are welcomed. Then don't dwell on them because they are just images like on a TV screen. This just happens to be the wrong channel. Go engage in something you love like spending time with your loved ones. YOU ARE NOT YOUR THOUGHTS.

Worrying/Racing Thoughts:

This for me was a serious behavioral pattern that I developed over many years. You don't see it as a problem really until it unravels you. Some things you should worry about because they may have a legit impact on your life, but most of the time we worry about outrageous scenarios. My plane is going to crash. If I go on this road trip with my friends we are going to crash. What if I go into this bank and someone tries to rob it? Basically, at every turn, you think your entire existence or the existence of someone you love is threatened. Is that really a way to live your life? You must really think you are special to think all these outrageous scenarios are going to happen to YOU! The truth is they won't happen. If they do then deal with them otherwise you're just ruining your days and exhausting yourself over something that hasn't actually happened in the real world.

It's funny because when these things don't happen, I somehow attribute it to my constant worrying. As if my racing thoughts of worry are the things that are preventing a tragedy from happening. This worrying then becomes a false safety net. It becomes the thing you rely on to protect yourself from bad things happening. There's a great quote I read once that opened my eyes to the sham that is worry. The Dalai Lama once said in his great book *The Art of Happiness* "If there is no solution to the problem then don't waste time worrying about it. If there is a solution to the problem then don't waste time worrying about it." If you can control the thing you are worried about then why are you worrying about it, fix it. If you can't control it then that is a great opportunity to flex your acceptance muscle and relinquish control on life.

I had to learn to relinquish at least some control of life. The only way I could do that was by trying the opposite. I would recognize when the worrying thoughts were happening and just see if there was a way I could solve the problem. If there wasn't then there was nothing I could do and I would do my best to let it go. It was hard but the more you do it the better you get at it and the more you realize that it's ok to not have control over things. If what you're doing isn't working then the opposite is at least worth a try. It's our belief that worrying is going to save us some future stress when in reality worrying is the stress right now. Worrying is useless because if you can solve the problem then you're good and if you can't then having some stressful thought and putting yourself through hell isn't helping anyone.

If you're afraid of flying but you've decided "I am going on this plane no matter what", then you've made your choice. Why do you start worrying about the flight when you book it two months before your trip? I've done this. I've booked a trip to Europe and for three months I was terrified of getting on that plane. Why? I am nowhere near that plane. If I decide to get on the plane, sit down, buckle in and take off, then maybe you can start worrying a bit. But anything up until the moment you are on that flight is useless. Also, once you are on the flight you aren't getting off it until it lands, so just flex that acceptance muscle and enjoy the ride.

Worrying and racing thoughts seemed to go hand in hand for me. The racing thoughts exacerbated the worrying and the worrying just made me panic and created more and more scenarios in my head. This is your snowball just continuing down that hill. You haven't really gotten out of the way. You haven't really stopped believing that not everything in your head is real. Next time your thoughts race, let them race and go do something you enjoy. Let's see where we go from here, yeah?

Follow Me

Hey you! Congratulations you've made it halfway through the book. That wasn't so bad was it?

Take a second and sign up for my email list here...

www.andrewcastro.net

I will not harass you with daily emails. The emails will come just once a week and here are some of the things you'll get:

New tips and insights on anxiety that aren't in the book

I'll be starting a podcast in October. You will get the episodes the day before they come out.

You'll be notified about public appearances and new products of mine coming out.

Look, you'll be seeing this page again at the end of the book so might as well just get it over with!

.

PART 2

WHERE DO WE GO FROM HERE?

Become a Scientist

I want to quickly preface part 2 of the book to help you get ready for the next 5 chapters.

The first is an understanding of basic human needs. Back in 1942, a Psychologist by the name of Abraham Maslow came up with Maslow's hierarchy of needs. The needs are as follows; Physiological, Safety, Love/Belonging, Esteem, and Self –Actualization. What I want to focus on briefly is the second one, safety.

Safety is an interesting thing because how do we know we are ever truly safe. The feeling of safety will be different for just about everyone. How you get to that point of feeling safe is entirely up to you. For me feeling safe was worrying about everything. It felt like my job, my responsibility to worry in order to make sure people would be ok. Or it was checking the locks on the door fifty times or brushing my teeth a certain way and then everything would be fine. It turns out everything was fine and no one got hurt during the time I had strong OCD. But chances are very likely that if I didn't do any of that stuff everything would've been the same if not better because I wouldn't have been driving myself crazy.

Life just unfolds and sometimes in strange ways. We can control some of it and can't control most of it. A lot of times feeling safe can be an illusion that you've created for yourself to feel, well, safe.

Your anxiety, like mine, in a weird way, is a safety net. We are afraid to let go of the fight because we feel the fight is keeping us safe. We think those worried thoughts are keeping everyone safe or even combing your hair a certain way keeps everything cool. It's not working, I can promise you that. Like every book that's like mine says "You wouldn't be reading this book if everything was working." But here you are. You've developed this bad habit that makes you feel comfortable. If you don't go against the habit then your identity can't be threatened and change can't get to you. I think we both know that is false because we don't live in a world where everything is the way we want it to be.

So for the next five chapters, I want you to become a scientist. What I mean by this is that I want you to experiment in the lab of your life with something new. Try and let go of the old ways, the ways that got you tangled in this mess in the first place. If you read a book like this and just go back to doing the same things that clearly don't work then you've wasted your time and money. All I'm asking is to try something new and not just for a day or week, but give it time. If you don't like what I have to say and the experiments in your lab go poorly then, by all means, send me a nasty email and give me a poor review on Amazon and move on to the next phase. But I challenge you to start experimenting.

CHAPTER 4

Stop Reacting, Start Acting

This is the part of the book where we discuss how to be proactive. You're whole life, or at least for a big chunk of it, you've just been reacting to things as they are presented to you. Not much thought has gone into your current state except maybe that you don't like it. I know for me, I never once gave a thought to why I got so angry so quickly, or why I worried so much, or why I was avoiding so many emotions that are just a very natural real part of life. It's time to stop reacting to things and to start applying yourself. Now you will see that most of what I mean by acting on things is basically doing what looks like, well, nothing. It'll make sense I kind of promise.

Recognize:

First and foremost I recognized my problems. Now of course by then it's usually too late and your snowball is in full speed. But that doesn't mean you can't destroy that snowball. Like I said earlier anxiety hates awareness. Bringing awareness and recognizing the issue is key. With awareness, we can now begin to start acting. You see your anxiety has been such a part of your unconscious life up until now. Just by reading this book you are completely aware that there is an issue that you need to understand deeper. Shining the light of awareness on your current state brings your anxiety out of hiding and into the sunlight. It is in this place that you can see things with clarity and rationally attack the problems. Now there are times when you start to truly become aware that you may think you are feeling a little worse than before. Don't let this fool you. This only means that you are feeling more, it doesn't mean you're feeling worse. When we face things head on the fear can intensify. Relish these moments because it truly is the start of your recovery.

Choosing:

This next one is very important. I remember so many times just trying to apply techniques with no real thought of where I was going. In my musical career, I have goals for myself. If you have goals then you consciously know what you're working towards (Disclaimer: One goal you should never put on yourself is a time limit. Everyone's anxiety is different and some people recover faster than others). What I mean by choosing is that you need to decide for yourself that you are going to be dedicated to becoming the person you want to become. This doesn't mean you can switch on a happy light and everything is all gravy. What it means is that from the moment you make this choice, you are dedicated and implement the practices to get you to where you want to go. You must have patience and genuine dedication. The great thing about being a human is that you always have a choice. After I made the decision that anxiety wasn't going to control me, I put my ass to the grind and made sure that it didn't. It takes time.

Choosing your path is so important because it gives you the confidence to take the next steps. You can't become what you don't actually want to become. I know that sounds weird because of course, we don't want anxiety. However, in your current state, you're not really giving yourself a choice. You have let your snowball run wild. Make that decision now! Don't just think about it. Start to put it into action. Words are weak. If I wrote this book but was still letting anxiety control every aspect of my life I'd be a fraud. Make a choice to act. Your state isn't going to change without any intent behind it.

Another thing I realized was that I didn't want to be the person I used to be. I wanted to be a new and better version of myself. Andrew 2.0 I always called him. I could see that person that I wanted to be. I knew it would be extreeeeeeemmmmly difficult to get there but I wanted it. I wanted it bad.

Allowing and Acceptance:

Let's get this started on the right foot. I know it, you know it, you have anxiety. You can't hide from that so stop trying.

Now I'm not going to sugar coat this part for you. This could be the toughest practice to implement. Allowance and acceptance are two very difficult things when we are facing suffering. Our first instinct always seems to be either to run or fight it. Both of these paths lead to the same thing. They both lead to frustration, fear, anger, and stress. If you don't face your anxiety then you'll always be afraid of it. If you constantly fight it and are angry at your situation, you'll create more stress and more panic when the feelings don't subside, which they won't.

There's a great analogy in Buddhist thought and I love it because it applies to me as a musician too. If the strings on your guitar are too tight then they won't play because they will snap. If the strings on your guitar are too loose then they won't play because they won't vibrate appropriately. You must find the right tuning somewhere in the middle. And of course everyone's tuning may be slightly different and that is ok. In fact, that is preferred or this world would be a very boring place.

Basically what this is saying is to find balance by not fighting and not running. By allowing the thoughts and feelings to be there we are giving them space. We are also showing that we are not afraid of these sensations and scary irrational thoughts. This is not easy because it goes against your normal behavior that you have become accustomed to. But then again those same behavioral patterns got you in this mess.

Here's a tip for you. Sometimes you have to fake it to make it. A lot of times I knew I was pretending to be ok with the anxiety but it was good practice and I knew that it must be done. When the anxiety started creeping up I would talk to it and say things like "Hey there you are. Come on in. Doors are open, make yourself at home." Is this actually how I felt? Absolutely not. I felt pretty awful but I wasn't going to be afraid of it anymore. However, the first time you do this you will probably notice that a tiny, little, very small amount of weight is lifted off your mind and body. That weight that you feel being lifted is the allowance and acceptance. You are saying to yourself,

"Hey this is ok, everything is ok". If what you have to face are these thoughts and sensations to get better... isn't that worth it?

Now what I am not saying is sit there and dwell on it. You don't need to get lost in it to show you don't care it's there. When it starts to creep up then talk to it. Let it know that it is welcome. Let it know that it can take all the time it needs. Your mind and body are trying to let this go but you won't let it. Trust your body and mind. Try something new. Try to allow it to be there. Give it permission to come on in and take a seat. After you recognize its presence take a breath, welcome it in and then go and engage in whatever you were doing or find something enjoyable to do. I promise that if you truly allow it to be there and accept that you have anxiety right now, you will feel a little relieved. After all, that's all it is...just a little anxiety.

Transforming the Fine Line:

Have you ever noticed that there isn't much of a difference between the feeling you get when you're excited and the feeling you get when you're afraid? I'm talking strictly about the feeling, not the mindset.

In your current state, you feel nervous or anxious and your mind immediately goes, "This is bad, how do I stop this? I want out of this!" Of course, by now you should know that the more you want something that can't go away to go away the worse it will get. Somewhere along the line while your snowball was building you developed the habit that this sensation is a threat to you. What if I were to tell you that you can transform that feeling into a more productive energy by developing a new habit? Would you like to do that? Don't answer that because it was a rhetorical question. I obviously know your answer.

That nervous feeling you get for no reason, maybe give it a reason. Perhaps that energy is just sitting there waiting to be focused on the right areas and used productively. So far you just habitually look at it with doom and gloom. That energy can serve a purpose in your life.

Next time that feeling starts to bubble up, catch it immediately. Shine some awareness on it and choose the way in which you want to act on it. Instead of just reacting in the same old way you've been reacting to it. Use it to focus deeper on your work or on a hobby you're passionate about. If you wake up with that feeling in the morning, use it to spark your days, "Let's go! Give me more of that energy! I need it to be productive today." It'll definitely feel fake at first but after a while, you'll see results.

Take a second and look at how many things in your life that are positive and productive but you view them in a negative light. If you run towards this ball of energy in you instead of away from it, you can transform it. We truly have the power to choose what something means to us, to dictate its influence on our lives. It's your perception of that nervousness and anxiousness that is the difference between making that energy productive and allowing it to drag you down.

Your Anxiety is Not A Special and Unique Snowflake:

Ok, so I kind of stole the title of this section from one of my favorite movies, Fight Club. (Which by the way is a great movie to watch and learn about letting go of possessions and who you think you are.)

Ok, a little tough love coming your way. I mentioned this earlier, and sorry, not sorry if I offend you, but your anxiety, though it does suck, is not special. If you think that you are the only one who is feeling what you're feeling, or suffering through internal struggles, you are just wrong. I discovered that in a way I was being a little selfish only worrying about how I feel every second of the day. I'm not saying any of us are selfish, egomaniacs. I'm just saying that when we fixate on our anxiety because it's such an infuriating problem, we can lose track of things that are truly important to us.

The universe doesn't owe you anything. The sooner you realize that things are just the way they are and sometimes they are shitty, the sooner you will learn to accept your situation. From that point on you can then decide who you want to be and how you want to get there. It's all up to you. But please realize your anxiety is not special. I've been so lost in my own anxiety that I didn't even realize close friends around me were suffering from the same thing and visa versa. We are all in this together, we all share some form of suffering. The quicker we can all realize that suffering is a part of life, the quicker we can master our response to that suffering. Basically, a much more gentle way of putting it is, you are not alone.

Another great quote from the movie Fight Club goes "The things you own, end up owning you." Right now your anxiety owns you because you have invested so much time and energy in it. By fighting it you have given your anxiety a reason to keep on living. The universe is a vast, amazing place. Hell, the world you live in is a vast amazing place.

Yet here you are narrowing everything down to a couple sensations and a few unpleasant thoughts.

Have a Little Spite:

This actually became one of my favorite things to do. I used to get terrified of going out. I would start to think that I was going to feel shitty at the bar with my friends or at a concert. Nothing really sounded like fun. But when I started to allow the anxiety to be there I started to get a little spiteful towards it, in a fun way. When a friend invited me out and I felt those thoughts creep up I would say to them "Hey, screw you, we are going out. You can come along if you want but we are definitely going to go hang out with my friends, sorry." I was done with anxiety controlling me. If I felt crappy then so be it. I wanted to do those things. I wasn't going to let anxiety make decisions for me anymore. This is my life, not anxiety's.

No Self-pity. Don't Wallow.

Do things that make you enjoy. This was something that really is a must. When you're stuck in the anxiety cycle and your snowball is out of control, we have a tendency to wallow and dwell on our situation. We also have a tendency towards self-pity. Self-pity is a very destructive quality that stems from anxiety. When we pity ourselves we justify our situation like why we aren't going out with friends or doing productive things with our life. It's tough to see through this because we are not sure what's on the other side. Instead, we wallow in self-pity because it makes us feel like our situation is special and important. There are 40 million people in this country facing some sort of anxiety. It's time to start realizing you are not alone and your situation is not special and that's a good thing. Our self-pity can be strongest when we are around loved ones. This will usually cause an outpouring of love and people feeling sorry for you. The love of family and friends cannot be denied and is extremely important in recovery. But receiving that support when you're in self-pity mode doesn't do much. Self-pity holds you back. Action through support moves you forward.

Stop the Fear of the Fear of the Fear of the Fear of the...You get the point:

Something I realized was that I wasn't even really having fear of anxiety anymore. Once the snowball sets off down the hill you start to fear the fear of having anxiety. That fear, in turn, creates the anxiety. It's a vicious yet kind of silly cycle when you think about it. You are fearing something that hasn't even happened. In a way, you are sabotaging yourself. I still do this once in a while. You'll be feeling great and relaxed and then you start to go "Hey where's the anxiety, I know it's coming." You are almost uncomfortable without the feeling of dread and worry. I always related it to those documentaries or films where the person is in jail for 20 years. When they get let out they don't know exactly how to live life in society. It's almost like they miss the security of the prison. Anxiety can be our cell. We think we are safe behind it but in reality, it is holding us back and controlling our lives. I always would remind myself and still do, "You're doing this to yourself." This is almost always a true statement. It really puts things in perspective when you say this to yourself. It helps click in the fact that you can choose a different way.

The fear of the fear can be just as real as the actual fear itself. So remember when you feel that fear or thought come up, allow it. Recognize it, engage it for a moment, maybe smile at it, then go about washing the dishes or watching your favorite show or playing guitar or reading a book.

Have Goals But with no Time Limits:

I believe in the power of setting goals. Goals give us the end before the beginning which can help pave the path we need to walk to get there. With anxiety, however, it's a little different. Sometimes with goals, you can give yourself a hard deadline to achieve what you're working towards. With anxiety, it's a little trickier than that. Anxiety patterns and habits take time to break and rebuild. It takes time to learn acceptance. Acceptance is like a muscle that needs to be trained over and over again. If you say to yourself on January first, "By February first I want all new habits and new thought patterns and all this anxiety to go away." That just won't fly in the anxiety world. In fact, this will just add more stress to your life.

Try just setting the goal of implementing allowance and acceptance and let the process unfold. The goal should still be to have an anxiety-free life where anxiety doesn't control your life anymore, but it's still a process more than a deadline. I found that my anxiety came off in layers. The more I implemented new habits and allowance and acceptance, the more I saw progress. The really bad times were just a little less intense. The racing thoughts started to slow down once the adrenaline wasn't as much of an issue. It became easier for me to start performing self-care tasks like meditation and going to the gym. The process gave me confidence and confidence leads to progress.

Two Steps Forward One Step Back:

Before you get all worried about the one step back part, let me explain. This is a huge part of the process. You're going to have times where you start feeling great. You'll notice those good times come in bunches. It started with one day of feeling better, then two in a row, then five and so on. But what you have to remember is that at the end of one of those bunches come a few bad days in a row. These are important opportunities. You must be diligent in your practice. Don't let the good days bring you so high that the bad ones ruin your progress. This is a very important part of your process. Don't let the bad days fool you. If you're having a bad day that only means you had a good day just before it ,otherwise how would know it's a bad day.

All Things Pass Including This:

At some level, we all know this to be true. However, I didn't truly understand it until I started reading books by Buddhist monks. This statement, when truly understood, not just intellectually, can change your perspective on everything, not just your anxiety. I've never met anyone who is constantly in a 24-hour cycle of anxiety. Everything comes in waves. We tend to not step back and appreciate the calm moments. We, and I mean people with anxiety, tend to think the calm is just the calm before the storm.

Try to appreciate the calm moments even if they seem to only last for a few moments. But truly begin to see, not just in your mind, but truly experience that everything passes.

Chapter 5

The Mind Makes A Great Slave But A Terrible Master

The title of this chapter is a quote I read a while back but isn't really attributed to one specific person. It is, however, a beautiful sentence. Another great quote is by the spiritual teacher Eckhart Tolle who said, "The human condition; lost in thought." I want to go deeper into thoughts in this chapter because I feel it's important to understand them better since they are the cause of so much trouble. We are going to get real trippy in this chapter. You may have to read this chapter a couple times to understand it. Or maybe I'm just not making sense. We will see.

Let's get one thing straight right from the start; you are never going to be able to stop having thoughts so stop fighting them. That is literally one of the main functions of your brain. Just like the heart pumps blood, the eyes see and take in images, the inner working of your ears hear things, your metabolism breaks down food into energy and of course, your brain conjures up thoughts and images and ideas in your head. These things are pretty much out of your control. What I just stated above is an important fact to understand because it truly helps you understand the nature of your brain. These functions that are out of your control are best left to their own devices in order to function properly.

The Thought Factory:

Just like your heart pumps blood, your eyes see, your ears hear and your digestive system...well you know, your mind's function is to produce thoughts.

Your brain is a factory and its main export is thoughts. All sorts of thoughts; Good ones, bad ones, evil ones, sweet ones, violent ones, perverted ones. Then "You", the conscious "You", react. You see your mind directs thoughts from deep down towards your awareness and from there you either latch on and give energy to whatever pops up or you can learn to let the bad unproductive thoughts go.

It is important to begin to understand that the nature and function of your mind is to think thoughts. Truly understanding, even if only intellectually, that your mind's function, like the other organs listed above, is just doing its job without your control. Where your control lives is in your extremely heightened awareness. Bringing your thoughts into your awareness allows you to see them for what they truly are, passing images. It's your instant, habitual reaction to them that makes them feel real and gives you that crappy emotional response you hate so much.

The reason why you feel so bad when you have a thought of hurting yourself or a loved one or that your life is going nowhere etc. is that you have zero space between the initial thought and your reaction to it. Your snowball has been built and you have habitually programmed yourself to believe that the little images in your head are your entire identity. This is something you need to unlearn. You can start by accumulating knowledge through reading books, talking with spiritual teachers or psychologists and through the art of meditation (Which I'll talk about later in the book).

The Rope and the Snake:

There's another Buddhist parable that relates to this. I'll paraphrase it. Basically, a person is walking on a dark road. Just in front of them, they see something on the ground. It appears to be a snake. They jump and scream and panic only to discover when light is shined upon the object that it is just a rope. Do you see how your mind can play these tricks on you? Your mind will take things and just run with it. The thought part of your mind doesn't care what is good or bad. It just collects data based on emotion, reaction or history and spews it back out. You can either choose to believe it with all your being or you can choose to take a different approach. The rope represents your thoughts. They aren't what they seem if you truly see them for what they are.

Don't let your mind fool you. The mind loves to play on your emotions and has what I like to call conceptualized vomit.

Ok, so this is sounding weird right? I hope so. Perhaps it is sounding strange because you've never really looked at your thoughts any other way than just believing what comes into your mind. There's good news and there's bad news. The bad news is you've probably been believing and thinking one way for a very long time. When you get depressed you start to think of other times you were depressed. Or you think of other people you know who are depressed. You may think that you are now one of those depressed people that have no joy left. You create ideas of who you think you are in your head. When you have anxiety and adrenaline pumping you have racing thoughts of what it means to be a crazy person. You think things like; "I'm going nuts" "I'm going to have to go to a mental institute". Sometimes you'll even conjure up images of movies or documentaries you've seen or patients you saw in hospitals that were mentally ill. The ideas and concepts are endless. Your mind has become your master. Whatever it says goes and you are at its mercy. I'll tell you from my experience, I was tired of my mind running my life.

So There is Some Good News:

You actually have two very powerful options at your disposal. The first is simply not believing that the images in your head are actual reality. You have this power. The same power that makes you aware of that thought in the first place, is the same power that you can wield to realize that a thought is just a projected image floating in your brain and it will soon burn out. The acceptance and allowance of scary thoughts takes away their edge. When you fight them or put all your awareness on these thoughts, they become your existence and your reality. This couldn't be further from the truth. It takes practice and time. You have to unlearn what you have learned as the great Jedi Master Yoda said. The simple act of recognition is such a huge start. When those thoughts come up instead of just reacting and falling right into their trap, pause for a second and think "Oh there's that crazy weird thought. Hey, crazy weird thought." And then let it do its worst and go on doing what you're doing. This does not mean we ignore the thought. It means we acknowledge its existence but that it is no more than that. That thought exists in your head because of the state you have got yourself in; it is nothing more than that. It is feeding off your current state of fighting or running. That simple recognition will give you so much power. It is the power of awareness. This leads to the other bit of good news.

One thing you can do is consciously transform your thoughts. Now what I'm about to say doesn't mean that when the thoughts come you get terrified and switch to thinking something that doesn't bother you. You need to acknowledge that scary thought very briefly and then you can transform it. I used to do funny, goofy things like making the thought into a playful cartoon. Or do something funny like turn the knife I had in my hand, in my thoughts, into a banana and now it lost all power. Then I'd just laugh and go about my business. Now, of course, you'll initially feel two things. One thing you'll feel is that you're faking it, which let's be honest, to start you are. But habits are broken through persistence. The second thing you'll notice is that the thought may still give you a lot of anxiety. You must learn to be patient and plant the seeds that you want to grow in the future. Through these methods, you are slowly but surely becoming the master and no longer the slave. Make your mind your bitch!

There was a story I heard of a doctor who had a patient that was terrified of being near open windows in tall buildings for fear he'd jump. So one day he and his therapist were walking down the hall to the office (The therapist's office was up high in a building) the patient started to become uneasy near the windows. One of the windows was open. The therapist stopped and looked at the window, then at the patient, and said: "Go ahead...jump." The patient had a wave of fear wash over, looked at his therapist curiously, and then was calm. The fear went away. As he went towards the fear of his thoughts of jumping they went away. Your mind doesn't care if things are good or bad it just feeds off the emotions you give it. It takes time but if you no longer buy into your thoughts they lose their grip on you. If you keep fearing your thoughts then you will continue to remain in the same cycle you're in. Make the unknown, known. Most of the things you fear you're not even quite sure why you fear them. So use the power of recognition instead of automatically getting lost in thought. Use your power of choice and choose not to buy into them. Instead of trying to run from the thought, welcome it and then go about your life making music, or eating dinner, or doing laundry or dishes. There is more to your life than a thought that exists only in your head, not in reality.

Chapter 6

Positivity Vs Productivity

I can't tell you how many books I've read where the main theme of the book is "More happiness right now!" Sure there may be some tricks and gimmicks that can give temporary bursts of happiness. But that is what those books fail to mention is that happiness, like everything else, is temporary.

In this chapter, I want to really show the difference between what positivity and productivity are. I'm also going to show you how negative feelings can be very productive...I'll bet you're interested now.

What is Positivity?:

Let me start off by saying that there is nothing wrong with being more positive in the way you think and act to an extent. There are a lot of benefits to finding positivity in certain situations. What I want to get you to change is thinking that, when you feel down or have a scary irrational thought, you need to somehow change that situation or thought into a positive one. Sometimes things are just shitty and it's OK!

Positivity to me is a general outlook on life, not on individual situations or thoughts. If you are using positivity for the immediate gratification of it then you are constantly going to be chasing a ghost.

Not everything is candy and rainbows (Not sure if that's an actual saying but I'm sticking with it). Sometimes life is challenging and difficult. If a loved one gets sick or injured you wouldn't just be like "No worries!" and start whistling as you walk away. Things can deeply affect us and they should if they are important. If you are feeling depressed and sad and burning with anxiety it's really tough to just pretend like everything is perfect and the way you want it. This is your life we are talking about. Just being positive with no bigger picture or goal in mind is fools gold.

Productivity:

When I talked about positivity as a general outlook on life I mean setting goals and having self-discipline. I'm talking about having a more positive nature to achieve productive goals and habits that will help you reach the optimal version of yourself. This book is about productivity. Taking steps forward and having a generally more positive outlook on your life as a whole will help you become an achiever and believer in what you set out to do.

Here's an example from my life and how I used big picture positivity to achieve more productivity with my anxiety;

When I found myself in this mess at first I just wanted out. I read those books about achieving happiness right now and you know what? I got that happiness. It lasted maybe a day and then I'd try something new. On and on it went. I'd feel down or anxious and try to just think about things that made me happy. In the end that's just avoidance behavior.

What truly got me to where I am now is deciding the person that I wanted to become and then working my tail off and being disciplined to achieve it. My positive outlook was based on the bigger picture I set for myself. By having that positive outlook on the whole I could start introducing new and productive habits that would give me the fuel I needed to become who I wanted to be. If I just took every individual crappy moment and tried to change it into a positive one I would be, and I was, so exhausted. I just accepted that at the time I had these issues, they were real and the only way to change them was to face them and change them and that would take time.

Again let me reiterate, it's ok to find the silver lining in certain situations. It's ok to try to look on the brightside sometimes. Just stop trying to control everything in search of some permanent blissful, happy state. What you want to find is balance. And nothing says balance like negativity. Am I right?

Negativity:

Let's just start off by saying you can't have positivity without negativity or how would you know you were being or feeling positive and visa versa.

Negative feelings and thoughts are always going to be with you, always. But something I learned a couple years ago really helped me take big strides in conquering my issues. Those negative times during your day or night when you feel sad, depressed and anxious are opportunities knocking at your door.

We grow and learn the most in our darkest hours. I mean you can't really grow much and learn when everything is candy and rainbows (See I'm sticking with it). It's like when a basketball team wins the championship, I'm sure raising that trophy feels amazing. But what about all the sacrifice and pain and training that went into it? The team would never know that feeling of bliss without the struggle to get there.

That struggle is what you are in right now. I know it sounds strange but you should relish these moments. Let the moments that feel darkest come and let that experience be your greatest teacher. Do you see now how something negative can be productive?

So next time those negative thoughts or feelings come up, accept them and learn from them. Don't dismiss them, or ignore them, or try to flip everything into some immediately positive feeling. That moment is there for the taking. So use it wisely and turn it into a productive moment for your future.

Chapter 7

Meditation And The Present Moment

Meditation:

I'm including meditation because personally, it has helped me the most with overcoming anxiety. Meditation is a powerful ancient tool that science has caught up to in the last 20 plus years or so. It has many proven benefits. What prevents people from trying meditation is that it is foreign to them and they believe they can't do it. Let me get one huge, gigantic misconception about meditation out of the way...YOU DO NOT HAVE TO BE ABLE TO STOP THINKING! THAT'S IMPOSSIBLE! I'm sorry I yelled at you but I had to get that off my chest.

The most common responses I get when I suggest meditation is "I don't have time" "Oh my mind races way too much I could never stop thinking" "It seems so boring what's the point". These are all valid reasons if you've tried meditation for a few months but most people say these things and dismiss it completely after a day or two. There's no sorcery behind meditation. There's no magic secret. You have to learn the craft and cultivate the right mindset through hard work and dedication. You can't meditate for four or five days and then not see results and just throw it out. Meditation is about training your mind to see your thoughts in a different light, in their true light. First I'm going to explain the simplest form of meditation and how to do it. Then I'll tell you how it has helped me.

Now explaining meditation isn't that difficult. The hard part, like anything, is remaining dedicated to it.

You want to start by finding a quiet place in your house that you can be as secluded as possible. Find a pillow or two and set them on the floor. You can also purchase real meditation cushions if you really want to pursue it. Now take a seat either cross-legged or you can kneel with your butt on the cushion. Settle yourself in and try and just let go of the stresses or problems that happened before you sat down and try not to think into the future where things haven't actually happened yet. This is your space to just relax and be truly present. Just like your bed is for sleeping, the meditation cushions are for being present.

All you have to do is close your eyes and begin to allow your body to breathe without trying to control it. Your body will breathe on its own I promise. Took me a while to get this but trust me your body will breathe on its own. Now begin to just be aware of where you are. Feel your butt on the cushion. Feel how your muscles and joints are bending in the position you're in. Now take your attention and focus it on a point at the rim of your nostril where you can feel your breath going in and out. The idea is to keep your attention there as long as you can. When you start to notice that your mind has wandered into some crazy thought about what you're going to eat for dinner, or some pretty girl or hunky dude you were talking to earlier on the most recent dating app, it is then that slowly but surely bring your attention back to your breath. You're going to repeat this probably 50-100 in your first sits. Don't kill yourself trying to keep it there. Just try and relax and focus your attention on your breath.

Now for the tough part. You won't be able to keep your attention on your breath for very long. If after your first sit you felt like you went 30 seconds or a minute without losing focus on your breath then you're probably not paying close enough attention. That's ok though, just relax. Remember the mind's job is to spew thoughts. This is called Monkey Mind and every beginner and even slightly advanced people have this. Your job while meditating is to notice those thoughts without judging whether you like them or not. Just notice they are there no matter how crazy they are and return your attention back to your breath. Start by just doing 3-6 minutes every morning before work and see how you feel. If you don't think you have time then wake up 3-6 minutes earlier than you usually do.

That's pretty much it. If you followed along closely you can see that meditation is a form of training. It's just like training a muscle. The more you catch yourself wandering in thought and return back to your breath you are training your awareness and improving your ability to not get caught up in the craziness that is thought. After a while this will become a new habit and the power of your awareness will overpower thoughts. You will begin to see that your thoughts only hold weight because you have the power to be aware of them and are choosing to give them power. Meditation will help you realize that you are aware and you can take back a lot of that power. One spiritual master named Sadhguru said that when he mastered the art of meditation it was like his thoughts were tiny cars stuck in traffic that he was watching pass from above in a hot air balloon and sometimes you can climb down into one of those cars and take it for a ride. Then when your are done with that car you can head back up to your balloon. That sounds peaceful, doesn't it?

I've been meditating for about two years now. I do it just about every day even if some days I just have time for 6-12 minutes. But they always say any meditation session is a good meditation session. Most of the time I wake up and drive over to the Buddhist temple I am part of and sit with a group from 8am-9am. I can truly attest to what dedication to something as powerful as meditation can do for your life. I've sat down and meditated when I felt I was having an anxiety attack. I wouldn't recommend that right away but when you get to a point where you're comfortable with meditation this can be a huge confidence builder. Meditation has taught me patience, which I bring to how I treat strong anxious sensations or weird irrational thoughts. It has taught me to be more present with not just myself but other people as well. I have become a better listener. I used to have horrible road rage and sometimes still do when people don't use blinkers and cut me off on the freeway and give me the finger and I just want to...ok and breathe. Sorry, I lost myself there. But seriously this ancient technique shows you what thoughts and sensations truly are and how they always, without fail, pass.

All I ask is you try it and stick with it for at least a month. Meditate every morning and night if you want to add an extra sit. Do it for one month. That should be about 25-30 sits or 50-60 if you're doing two a days. Give it a shot you have nothing to lose and so much to gain.

Side note: Two books I'd recommend getting are *Mindfulness in Plain English*, by Henepola Gunaratana and *Wherever You Go There You Are*, by Jon Kabat-Zin.

The Present Moment:

These days it feels like everyone, from your regular average Joe to elite athletes, are all trying to live in the present. But what does this mean and how can we benefit from it?

The present moment as I like to define it is simply the reality that is directly in front of you. Even when you think about regrets in the past or worries about the future you're doing that all in, yes you guessed it, the present moment. The past is gone and the future isn't here so everything is all happening right now. It is true that you are an accumulation of past moments but it has all accumulated to this moment. But it's also extremely important to remember how to best utilize that present moment. If you're just sitting on the couch going through the same old motions with your anxiety then it's not really going to benefit you. You must put that intent behind you. Your intent should be to move forward and to transform and eradicate your anxiety. So make sure to not just be present just for the sake of being present all the time. Be dedicated and disciplined in your practices and your implementation of new productive habits.

That is an important lesson to understand even just at the intellectual level. What I mean by intellectual level is that you understand the concept but maybe haven't learned how to truly live in it. Well, don't worry because millions of others are with you on that, including yours truly. Sometimes the harder you fight to live in the present the more your mind wanders into the past or stresses about the future.

One of the top three things I struggled with is drifting into the past, finding a moment or moments where anxiety deeply affected me and then taking those feelings and applying them to the future causing me to have anxiety about something that hasn't happened yet. It was a vicious cycle and still can cause me some problems. It became a daily habit. I'd feel the slightest anxious sensation or strange thought and my mind would instantly relate it to a past feeling I didn't like that caused me issues. Then I'd take that feeling and think "Oh no what if I have that again later today?"

"What if I can't sleep because I'll have these same thoughts and feelings?" It was like my mind was playing Ping-Pong. Just back and forth, back and forth never truly realizing that everything that was happening I was doing to myself by thinking I wasn't actually still in the present moment.

Now let me be clear. This does not mean you can't learn from the past or prepare and plan for the future. The great thing about our minds is that we can learn from mistakes and plan and sometimes predict the future. This is something that has helped us survive as a species. However, if you're reading this book you're probably not learning too much from your past. You're probably regretting a lot of it and fighting it. And as for your future, well you're probably terrified of it because you're afraid you'll be in the same position. While you're doing all of this you are in the present moment and you don't even know it. So take a breath and read this story that I'll paraphrase by Will Smith (No one saw that coming).

One day I came across this YouTube clip of Will Smith called "Fear". I like Will Smith so I went ahead and clicked. The story is about his first time skydiving. The night before he went out with his friends and one of them started talking about going skydiving the next day. Others chimed in and were pumped saying "Yeah man!" "I'm in!" Well Will Smith, a little hesitant and just going with the flow, showed his enthusiasm as well. When they parted ways to go to their separate hotel rooms he started getting really nervous. He felt he committed to something and now he was terrified. He woke up the next morning and couldn't really enjoy his breakfast he was so terrified. He went downstairs hoping everyone had changed their minds. That wasn't the case. They were all ready to go.

They made it to the site where they would take a quick training and board the plane. Up in the air, he was silent and nervous. The instructor/jumper he was clipped to walked him to the edge. He looked down, they counted one, two and then jumped. What he describes next is exactly what it's like to let go and walk straight into fear. Every moment leading up to the jump his head was already in the sky jumping. It ruined his whole night and morning. He felt miserable. Once he jumped and let go he said it was just pure bliss. There's a line in the video that resonated with me deeply. After he was done telling the story he said: "God puts the best things in life on the other side of fear." Whatever God you believe in or if you're Atheist or Agnostic or believe in energy or the universe, that line will ring true. Fear holds us back, fear lies to us, fear tricks us, fear wants to control us. We must see through the lies and deceit. Look at that the story Will Smith told and ask yourself what the point is of fearing something that hasn't happened yet. You can just not go skydiving if its that much of a problem. I mean it is reasonable to have some nerves jumping out of a plane but not to the point that it's going to ruin your night and morning. This applies to you and your anxiety and depression. The next time you wake up in the morning and start fearing having an anxiety attack or depression at lunch or dinner time, ask yourself, "what's the point of doing this?" Why not just let your day unfold and if anxiety comes or some depression comes then take it in stride and apply the other lessons of acceptance you've learned in this book.

You're Sabotaging yourself:

Anxiety sufferers are masters at sabotaging their present moment. You may actually feel totally fine in the moment and then you start searching for those anxious thoughts and feelings. It's become a habit. So when you aren't having those anxious thoughts and feelings you go searching for them because that's just what you know. It's ok to feel relaxed for a few minutes.

Don't set yourself up for failure. That anxiety that always comes at some point in the day, at this point in your journey, will probably be there anyway so why add any fear fuel to it. I can't stress enough to notice when you are sabotaging your present moment. Notice it and ask yourself if it is productive. Let me answer that for you, it's not. You have anxiety right now and there is no magic cure that makes it go away overnight. So accepting that is the first step to taking some of the fear out fearing your next attack or fearing having a crappy day. You may still have anxiety or depression but you'll take it in stride as it unfolds. I can guarantee you that by not sabotaging yourself you will take a huge load of fear off your shoulders. Don't sabotage your present moment.

Some Final Thoughts

Open Up:

People with anxiety disorders or whatever you want to call it are so stigmatized. People who have never experienced anxiety or depression on a consistent basis think that we are weak minded or fragile. On the contrary, the fact that you're here fighting (But actually not fighting right?!) and learning how to beat this thing shows how strong you truly are.

Don't be afraid to open up to friends and family about what you're going through. I was pretty brutally honest with friends and family, I may have scared some of them, but I knew they were there to support me through anything. Opening up to loved ones can really take some stress off your shoulders. When you start talking about your anxiety it takes the issues out of your little bubble and frames them in a new light. It puts them out into the world. Sometimes you'll find that hearing all your little problems out loud will make you chuckle at how weird some of them are.

Also don't be so terrified of the T word. That's right I'm talking about therapy. When you find the right therapist it can really open up your whole world. Everyone is different so you'll have to find the right therapist based on feel and the kind of progress you're trying to make. When I first went to therapy I was a little timid and that's ok. After all, it is a stranger you're talking to about deep personal issues. But it's kind of like stripping naked in front of a doctor, they've heard and seen it all. My therapist just kind of let things unfold. He would slowly ask me questions and in some ways let me dictate where the session was going.

I really encourage you to open up about what you're feeling and thinking. Bring it out of your body and mind and into the world. Having the courage to open up will help put things into perspective. Just try not to use it as a crutch. What I mean by that is don't rely on telling other people your problems to feel better about yourself. When you're struggling and need to talk to someone then that is ok but do it in doses.

Therapy also gives an outside perspective. It gives a chance for someone else, hopefully, someone who is highly credible, to examine what you're dealing with. It's like Tiger Woods and his golf swing. He's the best golfer of all time but he doesn't teach himself how to swing or correct all the problems with his swing. He has a swing coach come in and examine his swing from an outsider's perspective. We can't do everything on our own no matter how smart we think we are. It's like trying to be your own lawyer. Even lawyers don't represent themselves. It's ok to get help. It's ok to admit you have no idea what the fuck is going on!

Medication Good or Bad:

I'm not a doctor so I can't spend too much time on this. I can only tell you how I went about it and what I've seen with other people I know. Medication is a tool and when utilized correctly and responsibly can really help take the edge off and help you to implement new habits and patterns in your life. Medication, like Xanax or antidepressants, should be prescribed by a doctor, psychiatrist and used in conjunction with therapy. Medication by itself won't cure all your problems. Antidepressants are strong tools and can help change behavior. They can help balance you out when you're feeling sad or depressed and indifferent about life. But if you don't put in the work to plug in new habits then once you go off the medicine you will likely fall back into old patterns. Medication won't solve problems for you by itself.

I took Xanax for a couple months while I educated myself on my condition and went to therapy. What it did for me was give me a little room and space to work on building new habits. It would take that edge off to allow me to see a little more clearly.

After nearly two months I stopped taking it because I knew if I went any further with it then it would become a crutch. I used to take my bottle of Xanax on trips. It made me feel comfortable. But soon I realized that was a crutch too and I needed to grow and move on.

One day I was going on a trip just down to LA so it was only like an hour flight. I packed my pills but then stopped and stared at the bottle. I made the decision quick, like ripping off a Band-Aid, and unpacked the pills. I put them in a drawer and told myself that I was going to do this trip without them. I felt very nervous because I was going to be far enough away that if I really wanted a pill I couldn't get one. I can't tell you how much I grew from this. Now if you're on a prescription plan with your doctor then follow that. I got the pills on a street corner...just kidding. I got them for just general anxiety and wasn't on a strict plan just take as needed. So for me, I just made the decision that the pills weren't coming with me. I definitely had anxiety on the trip but I didn't care, or at least I couldn't care. It forced me to just get through it, to be in that moment with the sensations and thoughts without any relief. There was nothing I could do but let it pass. I came back from that trip and threw my pills away. My confidence was soaring at that point.

But I do want to stress that medicine is ok. I'm not knocking it. I believe in science! I just think that it can be thrown at anxiety patients with no plan. Medicine will not cure the problems you have but it can help give you space to implement the things that can. So don't think once you have a pill that your problems go away. You need to implement the same life-changing habits that you would do if you weren't taking the medicine.

Healthier Lifestyle:

A healthier lifestyle can help anyone in any situation. Consult a nutritionist and eat the right foods for your mind and body.

Finally get up and go to the gym. Work with a personal trainer to find the best workout plan for your body type and age.

Go out for a walk or run on a trail in nature. Humans need that connection to nature. We also need exercise so go kill two birds with one stone.

I'm sure you know what a healthier lifestyle can do for you. Now you just have to do it. Plus I needed to write another paragraph or two to get this book to 100 pages.

Afterword

Truth be told as I have been writing this book I do still suffer from some anxiety symptoms. But through discipline and belief, they just don't hold the same weight as they used to and I know that soon they will hold no weight. My mission in writing this book wasn't just to help you, the reader, but it was therapy for myself. I recently went through a break-up and I felt some of the old habits and symptoms pop up. But my dedication and confidence in my training and developing new habits has made me stronger. If I hadn't worked on myself the last two years I honestly think I would've broken down a long time ago and who knows where I'd be.

Anxiety is not something you need to carry with you the rest of your life. At least you don't have to carry it the same way you have been carrying it. I hate when people tell me to manage my anxiety. The only thing I'm going to manage is keeping myself on task and dedicated to eradicating old habits to shift my perspective on life. We got ourselves into this mess so we can definitely get ourselves out.

Live life without unnecessary fear. Stare your anxiety right in its ugly face and let it do its dirtiest work. Life is truly for living and anxiety is holding you back. That trip you've been putting off because you're afraid of feeling terrible on it, go ahead and book it and get out there and soak it all in. We truly only have this moment right now. So please stop reading this book at some point, give it to a friend in need and go live your awesome life. If you feel your life isn't awesome then start right now doing things you love that make you feel balanced and in harmony with everything around you.

I've honestly had some of the best trips of my life during my anxiety cycle. I went to Europe for three weeks even though I was terrified and depressed and couldn't sleep. I went on road trips with my friends to so many amazing places. I had anxiety the whole time. But in the deepest parts of my mind and heart, there was a little voice telling me, "you have to go on these trips, you have to live this life and not be afraid to live and die doing what you love." So far you've been living behind this wall of fear that you think is impenetrable. But I can tell you from experience, that wall of fear is made of glass that's just waiting to be shattered.

Well, that's it. I don't know how much more I can write without starting to bull shit you. It's time to start living. Check in with this book whenever you need to. At some point though, just like I did with my Xanax pills, you have to let this book go as well. I don't want this book to be your crutch. Read it and carry it with you for a couple months and then share it like I did with so many books that have helped me.

I would say I wish you luck on your journey but luck is something left to chance. You're going to grab hold of this thing and never look back!

Follow Me

Oh yeah! Way to go! You finished the book. It was super easy right?

Take a second and sign up for my email list here...

www.andrewcastro.net

I will not harass you with daily emails. The emails will come just once a week and here are some of the things you'll get:

New tips and insights on anxiety that aren't in the book

I'll be starting a podcast in October. You will get the episodes the day before they come out.

You'll be notified about public appearances and new products of mine coming out.

Made in the USA
Middletown, DE
19 February 2019